WONDER
STARTERS

Whales

Pictures by DAVID BULL

Published by WONDER BOOKS
A Division of Grosset & Dunlap, Inc.
51 Madison Avenue   New York, N.Y. 10010

About Wonder Starters

Wonder Starters are vocabulary controlled information books for young children. More than ninety per cent of the words in the text will be in the reading vocabulary of the vast majority of young readers. Word and sentence length have also been carefully controlled.

Key new words associated with the topic of each book are repeated with picture explanations in the Starters dictionary at the end. The dictionary can also be used as an index for teaching children to look things up.

Teachers and experts have been consulted on the content and accuracy of the books.

Published in the United States by Wonder Books, a Division of Grosset & Dunlap, Inc.

Library of Congress Catalog Card Number 74-2754
ISBN: 0-448-09679-X (Trade Edition)
ISBN: 0-448-06415-4 (Library Edition)

FIRST PRINTING 1974

Printed and bound in the United States.

This is a blue whale.
Blue whales are
the biggest animals in the world.

1

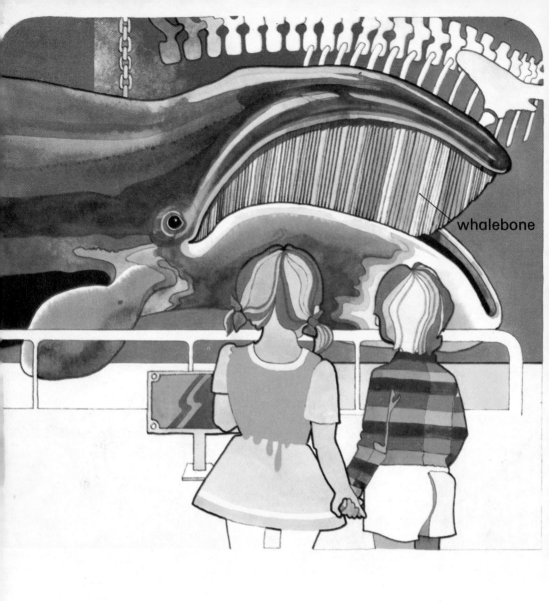

whalebone

This whale has a huge mouth.

2

krill

Blue whales eat small animals
called krill.
The whale sucks in water and krill.
Krill are caught in the whalebone.

killer whale

This whale has teeth.
It is a killer whale.
It eats penguins and seals.

4

narwhal

Another kind of whale
has a tusk.
Sailors used to sell the tusk.

5

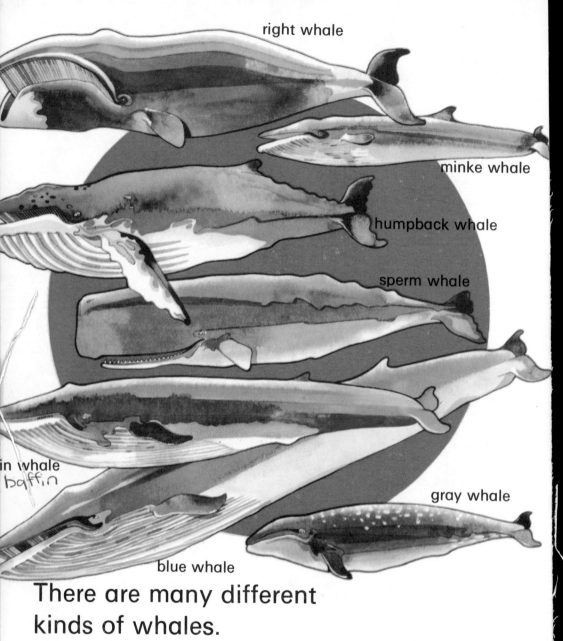

right whale

minke whale

humpback whale

sperm whale

fin whale
baffin

gray whale

blue whale

There are many different
kinds of whales.
Here are some of them.

6

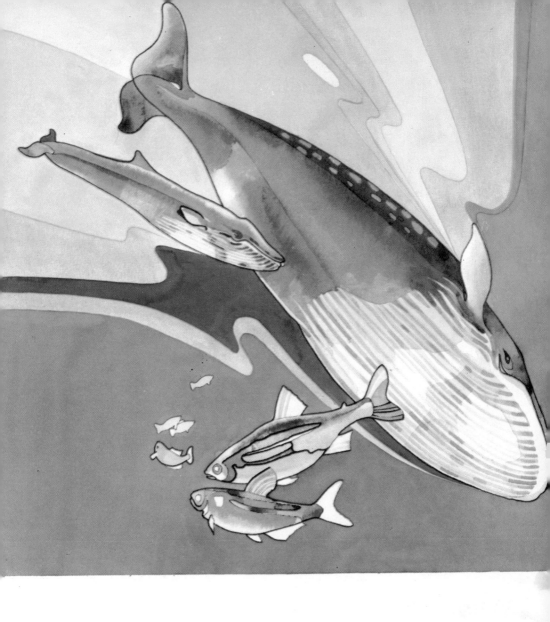

A baby whale drinks its mother's milk.
Here is a whale with her baby.

Whales look like fishes.
Fishes can breathe under water.
Whales must come up for air.

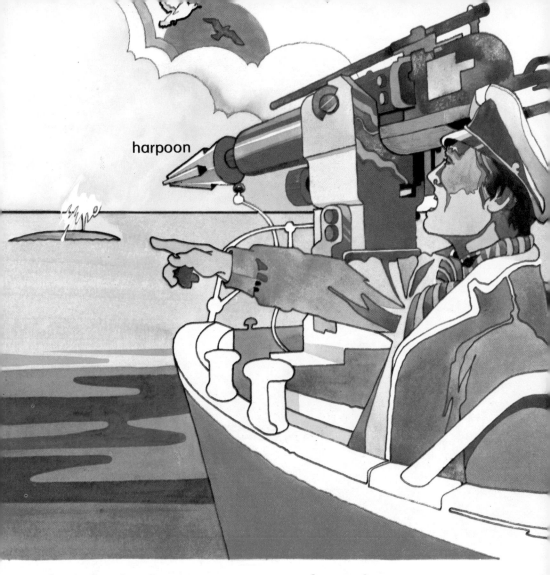

harpoon

A whale has come up for air.
This makes a spout.
Whale hunters see the spout.
They shout, "There she blows!"

9

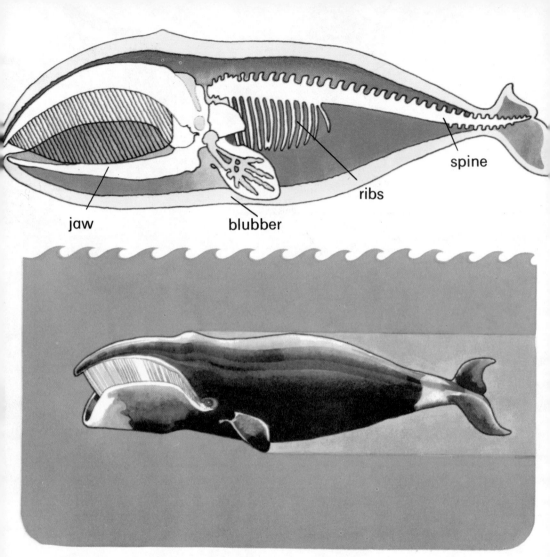

jaw

blubber

ribs

spine

Whales need to keep warm.
They have no fur.
They have fat instead.
The fat is called blubber.
10

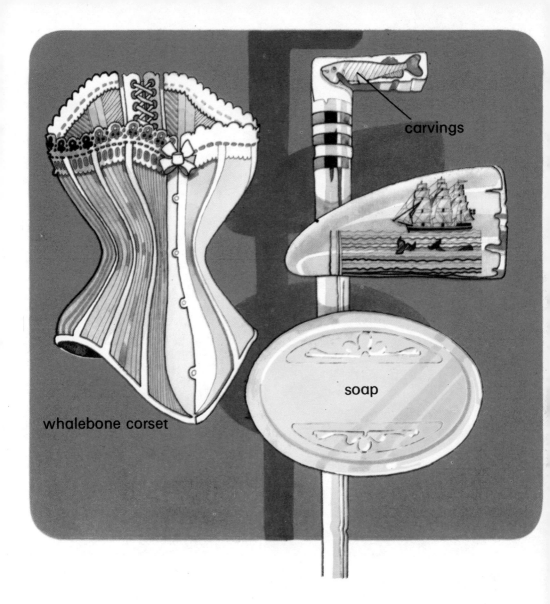

carvings

whalebone corset

soap

People hunt whales.
Once they used blubber for oil.
They used whalebone for corsets.

11

These are whale hunters of long ago.
They went after the whales
in small boats.
Many were drowned.
12

Nowadays, whale hunters use big ships.
Whale meat is used for food.

pilot whale

This is a pilot whale.
It is stranded on the beach.
Whales cannot live on land.
This whale cries for help.

Some other pilot whales
hear the cry.
They come to help.
Then many more get stuck.

Dolphins are very much like whales.
They are very clever.
They can do many tricks.
16

Scientists think that dolphins
talk to each other.
They are trying to learn
what dolphins say.

shark

These big fishes are sharks.
They may attack the dolphins.
The dolphins are driving them away.
18

This dolphin is sick.
He cannot get to the air.
The other dolphins push him
up to the air.

Sometimes dolphins
make friends with people.
They give children rides.
20

There are many old stories
about whales.
In this story the sailors thought
the whale was an island.

21

<u>See for yourself.</u>

Make a model of a whale from clay.

Paste paper over the clay.

When the paper is dry, paint your whale.

22

Starter's **Whales** words

blue
whale
(page 1)

penguin
(page 4)

mouth
(page 2)

seal
(page 4)

krill
(page 3)

narwhal
(page 5)

killer
whale
(page 4)

tusk
(page 5)

23

baby
(page 7)

fish
(page 8)

spout
(page 9)

whale hunter
(page 9)

harpoon
(page 9)

blubber
(page 10)
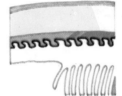

corset
(page 11)

sailors
(page 12)

ship
(page 12)

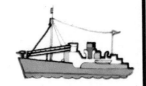

scientist
(page 17)

**pilot
whale**
(page 14)

push
(page 19)

dolphin
(page 16)

children
(page 20)

trick
(page 16)

island
(page 21)